Echoes of the Soul

Sneha Balani

BookLeaf
Publishing

India | USA | UK

Echoes of the Soul © 2024 Sneha Balani

All rights reserved.

No part of this publication may be reproduced, stored in a retrieval system, or transmitted, in any form or by any means, electronic, mechanical, photocopying, recording or otherwise, without the prior written permission of the presenters.

Sneha Balani asserts the moral right to be identified as the author of this work.

Presentation by *BookLeaf Publishing*

Web: www.bookleafpub.com

E-mail: info@bookleafpub.com

ISBN: 9789363314870

First edition 2024

To my late mother Sadhna,

my one and only true love,

Though you've journeyed beyond the earthly shore,

Your love lives on forevermore.

In every word, in every rhyme,

Your spirit lingers, an eternal chime.

Though you're gone, your love remains,

In every memory, it softly reigns.

With each page turned, your presence I feel,

Your love, a guiding light so real.

This book is for you, my dearest one,

Whose love shines brighter than the sun.

In the depths of my heart, you'll always stay,

My beloved mother, in every way.

In loving memory of Sadhna, my eternal muse.

ACKNOWLEDGEMENT

I am profoundly grateful to all those who have played a part in bringing this collection to fruition.

First and foremost, I extend my heartfelt gratitude to the readers who have embarked on this poetic journey with me. Your support and encouragement have been a source of inspiration and motivation throughout the writing process.

I am indebted to my family and friends for their unwavering belief in my creative endeavours. Their love, encouragement, and understanding have sustained me through the highs and lows of this journey. I would also like to express my appreciation to the publishing team for their dedication and expertise in bringing this book to life. Your passion for literature and commitment to excellence have made this project possible.

Last but not least, I extend my deepest gratitude to the muse within—the emotions, experiences, and insights that have inspired these poems. It is through your whispers and echoes that these words have found their way onto the page.

To all who have contributed to this endeavour in ways big and small, I offer my sincerest thanks. May these poems resonate with you and serve as a reminder of the beauty and resilience of the human spirit.

PREFACE

The collection you hold in your hands is a testament to the power of words to capture the essence of the human spirit. Within these pages, you will embark on a journey through the labyrinth of love and loss, guided by the tender touch of the poet's pen.

Each poem in this collection is a reflection of the author's own journey—a journey marked by moments of heartache and healing, of longing and hope. Through introspection and introspective exploration, the author invites you to accompany her on a voyage of self-discovery and transformation.

These verses are not merely words on a page; they are the breath of life, the song of the soul. They speak to the universal truths that unite us all—the ache of a broken heart, the yearning for connection, the resilience of the human spirit.

As you immerse yourself in these poems, may you find solace in the shared experiences of the human condition. May you discover the beauty of vulnerability and the transformative power of hope. And may you emerge from these pages, renewed and inspired to embrace the journey that lies ahead.

Ode to My Mother

Underneath the vast expanse of sky,
I count my blessings, soaring high,
For in this life, among the stars so bright,
You chose to hold me close, in love's sweet
light.

Forever bound, in a bond so true,
You're the one I get to call my mother, too.
From the moment I was cradled in your arms,
I found my home, safe from all harm.

You're my haven, my sanctuary, it's clear,
In your embrace, all worries disappear.
Your love, a beacon, shining bright,
Guiding me through both day and night.

You're my happy place, my heart's true song,
My pillar of strength, when days seem long.
Your laughter, like music, fills the air,
Your warmth, a blanket, beyond compare.

With you, I find solace, I find peace,
In your love, all troubles cease.
You've given me everything, I hold dear,
Your love, a treasure, forever near.

Thank you, dear mother, for all you've done,
For being my guide, my brightest sun.
Your strength, your patience, your gentle heart,
Have shaped me into who I am, in every part.

So here's to you, my guiding light,
My mother, my confidante, shining so bright.
I am me, because of you,
Forever grateful, for all you do.

Thank you to the one I love like no other,
My mother, my rock, my eternal cover.

Home

"I want to go home," I hear my heart whisper,
Where is home? I ask, with a quiver.
It's where everything's alright, it replies with
grace,
But where does such solace take flight, in what
space?

My heart's longing for a peaceful abode,
Searching for a haven on life's winding road.
But where is this haven, this sanctuary true?
Where everything is alright, where skies are
blue?

Home is not a place, my soul gently speaks,
It's not just the walls, or the floors, or the peaks.
It's the time and the people, the love that we
share,
It's the essence of life, floating in the air.

A place that feels like a tight hug, my soul adds,
Where worries dissolve, where the heart is glad.
Time stands still, just for a moment or two,
In the embrace of love, where dreams come true.

"Home is not where you are from," the soul
reminds,
"It's where you belong, where love binds.
Some travel the world, searching in vain,
While others find it in a person, in joy and pain."

Hope

In the whispers of the night, hope softly strays,
A silent prayer finding its way,
Like a beam of light in the darkest night,
It harbours the promise to make things right.

It whispers, "It's over, you'll rise once more,"
And with its touch, disdain it shall shatter,
When tears have run dry and dawn breaks anew,
Hope smiles, embracing skies of blue.

It unveils the strength within your soul's deep
core,
Nurturing wounds, by your bedside it'll stay,
A friend's gentle voice in the tempest's roar,
A mother's embrace, chaos it'll allay.

A promise unspoken, of tomorrows bright,
For hope births beginnings from sorrow's night.

Healing

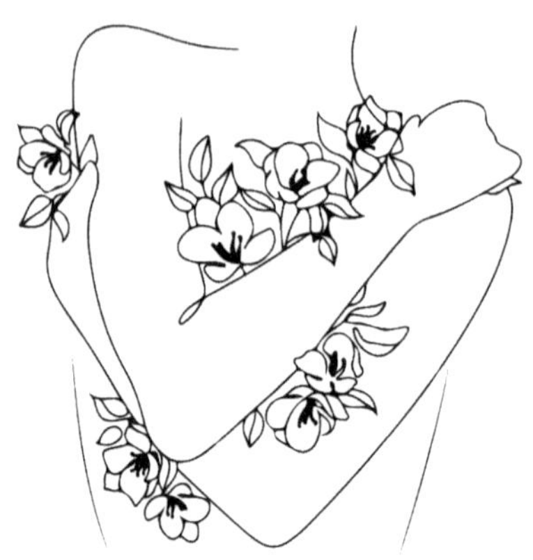

In the realm where healing springs,
A journey dances on unseen wings.
One day, pain seems a distant song,
One day, you believe the hurt is gone.

One day, you sense you've left him behind,
Yet, echoes linger, subtle and unkind.
As your pillow stays dry, a silent vow,
A name, a song, a walk, a rain somehow,

They beckon back the ache, the strain,
Undoing efforts, rendering in vain.
Clouds of sorrow gather, skies of grey,
Tears cascade, like rain, they find their way,

Upon that pillow, where dreams refrain,
Let the storm cleanse, let the tears explain.
For healing, oh, it jests and jests,
Etchings on the heart, it gently tests.

Seasons of rain, it takes to undo,
But with each tear, a new dawn anew.
Rise once more, with courage, with grace,
Through every trial, every tear-traced place.

For in the rhythm of healing's refrain,
Lies the courage to dance in the rain.

Hurt

"Hurt"
Hurt is but a four-letter word they say,
"Did it Hurt?" They ask, in a trivial way.
But what I feel is not that small,
The word can't capture, can't express it all.

It's deeper, darker, than mere "hurt" implies,
An endless fight, where pain never dies.
Destroyed, obliterated, desecrated, true,
Annihilated, demolished , my soul askew.

Shattered, demoralised, left me to stall,
But "hurt"? No, it wasn't that small.
It carved my soul, night and day,
A tempest, a whirlwind, that swept me away.

So don't reduce it to a mere "hurt",
It was a storm, a chaos, leaving me inert.
For what I felt was more than a word,
It was anguish, it was pain, it was a world.

Strength

In the depths of my soul, a silent battle rages,
A tale of strength born from the cruellest cages.
Believe me when I whisper of the trials I've
faced,
Of innocence lost, and scars that can't be erased.

I wasn't always the warrior you see before you
now,
Once a tender spirit, trusting, wondering how
Every hand I grasped, seemed poised to wound,
Every promise shattered, every trust marooned.

Those I held close, they took more than they
gave,
Leaving me broken, struggling to be brave.
Attacked by those meant to shelter and defend,
Left me wondering when this nightmare would
end.

So believe me when I say, strength wasn't a
choice,
Forced upon me by circumstance, I found my
voice.
Picking up the shattered pieces, each shard a
bitter sting,
I forged ahead, refusing to let despair take wing.

No longer do I offer my trust or hand to hold,
Fearful of the pain, the stories left untold.
I walk this path alone, with fists clenched tight,
Each step is a testament to my relentless fight.

But beneath this facade, this armour I wear,
Lies a heart still tender, burdened by despair.
Alone in the night, I let the tears flow free,
A moment of vulnerability, just between me and
me.

So let me be both warrior and child,
In this dance of strength and tears reconciled.
For within the depths of my weary soul,
Lies the truth of a journey, making me whole.

Choices

May courage be your constant guide,
In choosing yourself, never to hide.
Moving forward, with each new day,
Embracing growth, come what may.

Step out of comfort, into the unknown,
For there, your true potential is shown.
Know your worth, amidst the doubt,
Your heart deserves to sing and shout.

Each morning brings a fresh start,
With hope in your soul, and dreams in your
heart.
Think beyond the ordinary, reach for the sky,
For in chasing your dreams, you'll learn to fly.

Progress isn't easy, but worth the fight,
Each obstacle faced brings you closer to light.
Make the most of every moment, every chance,
For life is a gift, a joyous dance.

You are worthy of success, of all things grand,
Deserve the triumphs, you've worked to
command.
Believe in yourself, in all that you do,
For you are worthy, through and through.

Solitude

In the quiet of the night, with shadows deep,
You keep the lights on, afraid to sleep.
Alone in theatres, you dare not go,
Missing out on movies, ice cream, and more.

Two scoops too much, two flavours not enough,
Simple tasks like these, made tough.
Fearing sickness, for chicken soup alone,
And doctor's visits, with hand as your own.

Yet amidst these fears, there's a silent shift,
In solitude's embrace, a subtle lift.
The blanket all yours, no need to share,
And popcorn abundance, a secret affair.

Mastering the soup, with tender care,
Finding solace in walks, in the open air.
Tightening shoelaces, stepping outside,
Embracing your own company with pride.

You're doing good, my dear, don't you see?
In the quiet moments, finding glee.
So don't stop now, keep pushing through,
Discovering strength, discovering the new you.

Kintsugi

In a world that spins with haste and fury,
All we need is kindness, really,
A gentle touch, a tender heart,
Someone to kiss our wounds without seeing the
scars.

Have you heard of kintsugi,
The Japanese art, profound and wise,
Repairing broken things with gold,
Making them more beautiful, more bold.

Kindness is the gold, warm and bright,
That repairs broken souls, restoring light,
It fills the cracks with love and care,
Transforming pain, making it rare.

This time, I hope, with all my might,
Someone looks at me with kind eyes,
And offers the gold to repair my soul,
To make me whole, to make me whole.

Someone who sees the beauty in my pain,
Who says, "You are broken, but beautiful,
again."
For in the fragments, in the cracks,
There lies a story, a treasure, a pact.
So, let kindness be the art we share,
Repairing each other with love and care,
For all we need is kindness, really,
To kiss our wounds and see us as lovely.

Grief

Grief's Journey

Grief, a journey through shadowed lands,
A path where sorrow gently stands,
Through stages vast and depths unknown,
In heart's deep silence, seeds are sown.

Denial's Whisper

In disbelief, the heart first lies,
Shielded by denial's disguise,
"I cannot bear this loss," it sighs,
A fragile hope in tear-stained eyes.

Anger's Flame

Then anger burns with fierce disdain,
A fire to mask the inner pain,
"Why must I bear this cruel strain?"
In wrath's embrace, all joy seems slain.

Bargain's Plea

In whispered bargains, solace sought,
"If only," cries the desperate thought,
A dance with fate in webs tight-wrought,
Seeking to change the pain life brought.

Depression's Veil

Depression casts a shadow deep,
In silent rooms, where sorrows seep,
A heavy heart, no will to leap,
In quiet tears, the soul does weep.

Acceptance's Dawn

But time, it heals with gentle grace,
Acceptance dawns, a new embrace,
"In loss, there's love no time can chase,"
A peaceful smile on a tear-streaked face.

Grief, a journey marked by strife,
Yet through its stages, blooms new life,
In memory's hold, love shines bright,
A testament to love's true light.

Through shadowed lands, we find our way,
From night to dawn, from dark to day,
Grief's tender path, though steep and grey,
Leads hearts to heal, to hope, to stay.

Maybe

In the tapestry of our lives, mayhaps we find,
Healing threads, woven from firsts to lasts
entwined,
May be from losses mourned, friendships torn
apart,
And hearts broken by love's cruel dart.

Perhaps there's no destination, no end in sight,
For healing's journey knows no upward flight.
It staggers through love's tunnels deep,
In the shadows of loss, where memories keep.

Maybe our healing's not a static state to achieve,
But a voyage forward, where we must believe,
In moving onward, away from pain's hold,
Towards shores of growth, where new stories
unfold.
Not to erase the past, but to carry it along,

As lessons learned in life's vibrant song.
To embrace the pain, let it reside,
Within our hearts, as wisdom's guide.

Maybe, just maybe, we've been running astray,
From the treasures meant to light our way.
Tools of resilience, burdens turned light,
Guiding us through life's darkest night.

So let us not flee, but hold on tight,
To the things that shape us, through day and
night.
For in their weight lies strength untold,
In the adventure of life, they're worth more than
gold.

You belong

In this big stage of life's embrace,
May you find souls who lend you grace.
People who make your heart sing,
Where you fit perfectly, every string.

May their presence calm your storm,
Their essence, a shelter, safe and warm.
Surround yourself with hearts so true,
Where every moment feels brand new.

For in their company, you'll find,
A sense of belonging, one of a kind.
Yet amidst the crowd, don't forget,
The love within, your own mindset.

Know that you belong, always and forever,
In this world's dance, never say never.
So cherish each moment, every day,
For you're meant to be here, come what may.

You are enough

In shadows, when doubt itself looms,
Remember, dear soul, you're enough in the
rooms
Of your heart's quiet ache, where doubts start to
creep,
You're still worthy, dear one, even as you weep.

On days when the sun hides, and clouds weigh
you down,
When you'd rather stay hidden, wearing a frown,
Know this, precious being, in each step you
tread,
You're enough, even if you'd rather stay in bed.

When love leaves a scar, a wound that won't
heal,
And trust feels like shattered glass under your
heel,
In the midst of your pain, though it may seem
tough,
You're still worthy of love, for you are enough.

Facing the mirror, unsure of your face,
Doubting your worth in this chaotic race,
But listen, my dear, in your reflection's view,
You're enough, just as you are, through and
through.

In moments of chaos, when time slips away,
And tasks left undone haunt the end of the day,
Even then, weary soul, as you catch your breath,
You're still enough, despite unfinished steps.

You are always, forever, more than you know,
A spark in the darkness, a steady glow.
So be kind to yourself, in each moment, each
phase,
For you're enough, always, in countless ways.

Trust The Journey

When choices stand tall and paths diverge,
Doubt may creep in where clarity used to surge.
A heart once firm now feels the strain,
As the winds of change blow in like rain.

At life's great junction, where we decide,
Imprints on the soul can't be denied.
Sadness may follow, confusion may bloom,
But trust in the journey, let go of the gloom.

Each new beginning requires an end,
Old fears will break as new hopes mend.
Through the night of uncertainty, you may roam,
Yet stars of your choices will guide you home.

Embrace the rhythm of days anew,
Welcome the confusion as it helps you to grow.
Uncertainty is just part of the game,
As you carve out your future and stake your
claim.

Believe in the process, the wisdom within,
Let your heart's compass steer you again.
In the realm of decisions, both heavy and light,
Your spirit will lead you from darkness to light.

Whispers of a weary soul....

She feels tired, deep in her soul,
Not just her body, but something whole.
It's like she's been running from unseen fears,
From the truth that's been building over the
years.

Her life isn't what she hoped it would be,
She blames herself, and can't set herself free.
She dreams of a life that she'll never know,
And in her mind, peace doesn't grow.

No voices haunt her, just a quiet dread,
A storm is coming, she feels it ahead.
It might break her down, leave her in parts,
But from those pieces, she'll find new starts.

Lost in tomorrow's shadow....

I've realised something deep inside,
I'm not living, just along for the ride.
Each day passes in a blur,
Waiting for tomorrow, but not sure.

My life revolves around what's next,
A future that's always perplexing.
I'm waiting for something, not knowing what,
And that unknown ties my heart in knots.

Burdened by birth....

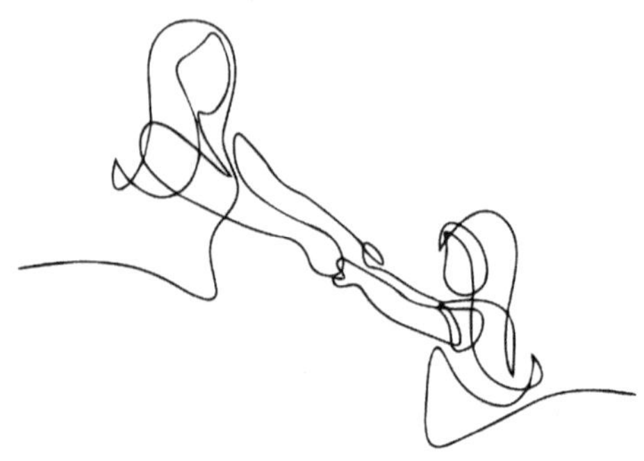

I wonder how it feels to grow
Unwanted since your earliest breath,
When whispers warned your mother so,
Yet she chose you, defying death.

Her life turned harder, dreams erased,
For your small sake, she bore the weight.
A world of disrespect she faced,
Her struggle, endless, sealing fate.

As a child, you hear the blame,
That you, the cause of all her pain,
How do you shed that haunting shame,
The guilt of birth, a cruel chain?

Her love is mixed with deep regret,
Her anger spills, she can't conceal.

No father's warmth, just cold neglect,
The wounds from which you cannot heal.

You strive to be her saving grace,
A strength that barely holds its own,
A hollow cup in endless race,
To fill a void, to mend what's torn.

As the eldest daughter, you must stand,
A mother when your own isn't there,
A provider with no helping hand,
A sister's shield, a soul laid bare.

No love to lift you from the night,
No solace, just survival's fight.
Forever guilty of your birth,
A weary soul who's lost her worth.

I am afraid

I am afraid of attachments and people leaving
me behind,
In the depths of loneliness, where solace is hard
to find.
Alone in the void, where shadows dance,
I fear losing connections, taking a chance.

I am afraid of the intensity of my love,
Unreturned, it seems, like a mourning dove.
Vulnerable I stand, amidst unspoken dreams,
Yearning for reciprocation, or so it seems.

Shaking hands, a body's tremble, a heart's
painful storm,
Numbness spreads, in silence, taking form.
A symphony of fear, echoes in the night,
I am afraid of losing the fight.

To be called weak, a label I dread,
Yet in vulnerability, strength is often bred.
In the shadows, where comfort resides,
I am afraid of the darkness that hides.

Yet in facing fears, we find our might,
In vulnerability, we stand upright.
Embracing the unknown, with courage we see,
I am afraid, but I'll set myself free.

I crave softness…

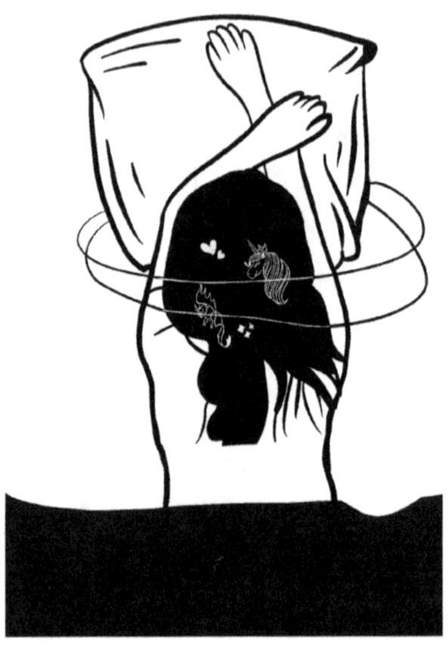

I crave a gentle life, a serene refrain,
For I've glimpsed hell's relentless domain.
No need for harsh lessons, I implore,
Give me evenings soft, sweet to the core.

Nights draped in comfort, like wool so fine,
Let laughter overflow, tears intertwine.
Beside those who effortlessly care,
Loving us deeply, beyond compare.

I long to breathe the air of dreams untold,
To make memories in lands of old.
Though hardships shaped me, both painful and
bright,
I seek days abundant, filled with light.

I aspire to be formless, to flow with ease,
Like water or lava, as each day sees.
Both sides, honest, both parts of me,
All versions valid, all identities free.

In being true to myself, I find sanctuary,
Prefer a few close bonds, deep and unwary.
Acceptance over acclaim, my creed,
In being there for others, I find my need.

To be the solace, the guiding light,
To be for others what was missing in my night.
Softness born from the harshest cold,
A strength in vulnerability, I proudly hold.

Unbroken by trials meant to rend,
My light shines forth, an unyielding blend.
Together, we radiate, a constellation bright,
In embracing softness, we find our might.

The Truth of Life and Death

We trust in life's unfulfilled promises,
Cherishing it deeply, believing sincerely.
It paints rosy visions of what could be,
Yet rarely fulfils these fantasies.

We are enticed, feeling there's so much more to
come,
But life deceives, breaks hearts, and steals our
treasures.
Still, we cling to its enticing lies.

Death, in contrast, makes but one vow:
One day it will come, freeing us from life's
deceits.
Death is the faithful friend,
with no false promises or illusions.

Death is the only truth;
all else are paths to our ultimate destiny.

A Silent Cry of the heart....

Each morning I rise with a sigh,
Death, unkind, won't answer my cry.
Counting moments, hours to the end,
Hoping night will mercy send.

A heart weighed down,
no respite found,
Expectations' chains tightly wound.
Loneliness, my shadow, stays,
Companion through all my days.

We share the meals, the silent room,
Together in this constant gloom.
If I knew better, it would be clear,
Loneliness, my love sincere.

Every day, I strive to feel,
To shake the numb, to heal, to heal.
But like a plant without care,
My soul wilts, roots laid bare.

Only death offers a sweet release,
A promise of eternal peace.
When it arrives, a loving guest,
I'll hold it close, find my rest.

Life, a bully, harsh and cold,
With death's embrace, I'll be consoled.
A shield from pain, a gentle shroud,
In death's arms, I'll be proud.

Beyond mixed signals....

You can't fight to be loved by someone,
Love that's real won't be outrun.
If they care, they'll hold you near,
Fight your battles, quell your fear.

Confusion clouds where love should light,
In their push and pull, there's blight.
If words they speak trouble your mind,
Their actions, too, are not aligned.

Actions louder than words can say,
If love is there, it finds its way. In eyes,
if warmth you cannot see,
The truth is hard: it's not to be.

You want to give the benefit of doubt,
Think time will turn their heart about.
They need more space, you're pushing too much,
Or maybe start as friends, just as such.

But if signals mixed cause you pain,
And kindness turns to hurt again,
Negative energy fills your days,
It's time to part, find different ways.

Trust me, love can't be chased or forced,
If it's true, it flows its course.
To force love's hand is all in vain,
For true love never brings such pain.

Walk the path, but know your worth,
In love that's real, you'll find your berth.
No need to chase, no need to flee,
For love that's true will always be.

Gift of a fading light....

Sometimes I wish I could give away this little
life,
to someone who'd stay with purpose clear, with
dreams so bright,
A reason to face each endless night.

I feel so small, adrift and lost,
My hopes and dreams have paid the cost.
If I could trade my weary soul,
For someone who feels whole.

Their joy would bloom where mine has waned,
In a heart that isn't stained.
Perhaps my life, so worn and frail,
Could help another's spirit sail.

In giving what I cannot keep,
I'd find a peace, a final sleep,
Knowing someone else could find
A meaning that I couldn't find.

Forged by Shadows

The greatest healer has been wounded deep,
Their wisdom born from nights of restless sleep.
The deepest lover felt their heartbreak wide,
Their boundless love emerging from inside.

The conscious being wandered, lost in night,
Their clarity discovered through lack of sight.
Though pain and darkness carve our weary
souls,
They shape our journey, making us whole.

Whether we like it or not, it's true,
Our wounds and scars reveal a brighter hue.
In the depths of sorrow, we find our way,
Pain as our guide, illuminating day.

Darkness and trials, our greatest teachers be,
They mould and forge us into who we're meant
to be.
Through suffering's grip, we rise and
understand,
Embracing our path, we firmly stand.

For in the shadows, our strength is found,
Our spirits lifted from the ground.
Initiated by the struggles we face,
We step into our power, full of grace.

So let the wounds and darkness play their part,
For they are the keys to an awakened heart.
In the dance of shadows, we find our light,
Emerging from the depths, ready to take flight.

The Cleansing Tide

A healing stage is disgust, indeed,
A bitter taste, a heart's true need.
You will be disgusted, deep inside,
By those whose love you sought with pride.

Embarrassed by the choices made,
By those who touched your soul, then strayed.
Feel this feeling, let it rise,
A truth unveiled, a new sunrise.

Yes, let disgust wash over you,
A cleansing tide, a pain that's true.
For in this wave, a lesson learned,
A path to self-respect is earned.

Let it go, release the past,
This feeling fades, it doesn't last.

That will never be you again,
Rise anew, free from the pain.

Embracing Purpose

What's the purpose of our fight?
Why do we face these daily wars,
Battling demons, closing doors?
Our purpose is to accept this life,

To rise above the daily strife.
This human form, a gift to tend,
Our own true self, our closest friend.
Nurture it with tender care,
Protect it from the world's despair.

Cherish, nourish, give it grace,
Fill it with the best embrace.
Love it deeply, heart and soul,
Make it vibrant, make it whole.

Give it all the joy it needs,
In loving it, our purpose feeds.

Steps of faith

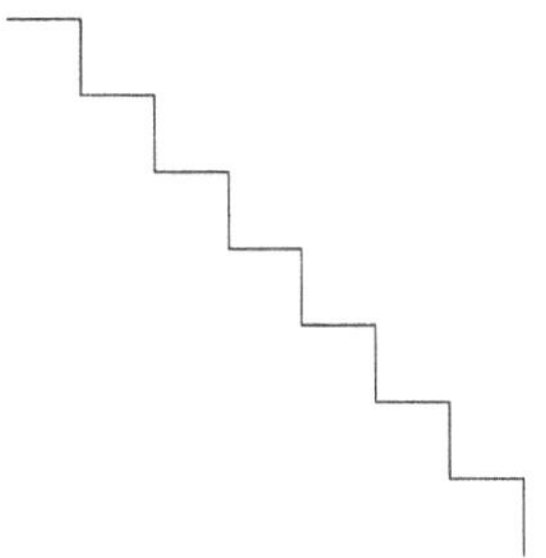

Loving someone is like climbing temple stairs,
Unsure if we'll find divinity there.
Yet with each step, our hearts remain true,
Embarking on faith, both me and you.

In the climb, hope's light leads the way,
Trusting the journey, come what may.
For in love's ascent, faith is our guide,
Whether we find god, or just each other, inside.

Love's Inner Compass

When heartache knocks and tears begin,
Remember this, to look within.
The culprit here is not the pain,
But ignorance of the mind's own chain.

Unseen, we cling to what we see,
In every smile, in every plea.
Our minds so strong, attachments grow,
To things that barely even know.

Awareness is the first step, my friend,
To understand, to comprehend,
How easily we give our heart,
To fill a void, to mend a part.

But know this truth, so often missed,
Our true self, Love, does exist.
We seek it out in others' care,
Yet find it's always been right there.

No person, object, love displayed,
Can fill the space where dreams have strayed.
The ocean deep of love, so vast,
Exists within, the shadows cast.

To find this love, look to your soul,
For only you can make it whole.
Attachment shrinks your world, you see,
But love with grace, and you'll be free.

Love everyone, but do not cling,
Let freedom be your heart's own wing.
For love's a gift to give and share,
Without the need to hold or snare.

In knowing self, in Love's pure light, you'll
navigate the darkest night.
So when breakup's pain you face
Look within and find your grace.

Light within the Shadows

Shadows deep where sorrows lay,
I used to think there'd be no day,
That some are bound to endless pain,
And sunshine never would grace again.

But time has shown, as days unfold,
A secret truth, a light to hold.
For even in the darkest night,
A glimmer sparks, a hopeful light.

With patience, wounds began to heal,
A strength arose, once faint, now real.
Each step, though small, a forward tread,
A brighter path where once I bled.

Though hurt may linger, echoes vast,
I'm not the shadow of my past.
I've grown in ways both seen and felt,
In fires of pain, my spirit smelt.

I've learned to face the storms that roar,
With courage built from trials before.
No longer chained by doubts and fears,
I've woven strength from fallen tears.

In moments where I felt the same,
Hurting, breaking, lost in blame,
I see now how I've truly changed,
In countless ways, my soul's arranged.

For now, I hold a power new,
A love for self, both strong and true.
A faith that time does heal and mend,
A journey that does not descend.

I found the light within my core,
A beacon when I felt no more.
And through this love, a self-embrace,
I carved a path to a healing place.

So here I stand, with hope alight,
A testament to inner fight.
For though the battles raged and tore,
I learned to love, and found my shore.

Beyond the Facade....

Why do we silence cries of pain,
Dismiss the tears that fall like rain?
We mask our hearts, deny the strife,
Pretend we're living a perfect life.

Encourage others to ignore
The grief that shakes them to the core.
Normalcy, we quickly chase,
Yet wounds remain, time can't erase.

Betrayal's sting, a silent scream,
Love's shattered trust, a broken dream.
We urge them on, to move ahead,
To bury all the words unsaid.

Failures faced with unseen scars,
We watch from distant, lonely stars.
Our fables filled with love's embrace,
Yet seldom shown in human grace.

Society's facade, so bright,
Casts shadows deep, obscures the light.
In trying hard to fit within,
We lose ourselves, our truth grows thin.

Amid the dark of loss and death,
Where unkindness steals the breath,
A spark of hope still flickers through,
Reminding us the good is true.

Feel the fear, embrace the real,
Let hearts be heard, let souls reveal.
In shared sorrow, find the way,
To bring the dawn of kinder day.

Learn to let go

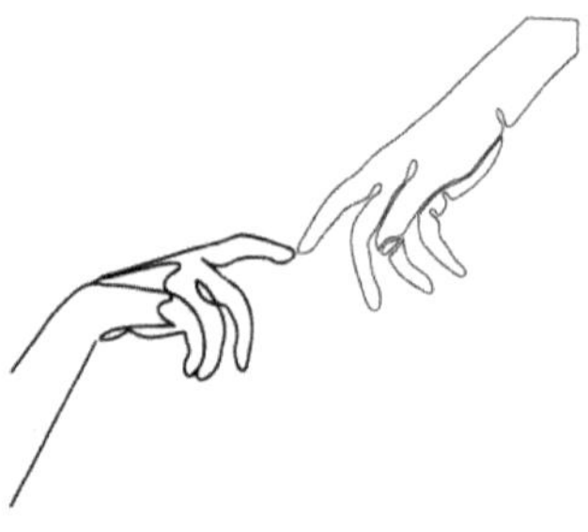

Sometimes dreams must be released,
Plans set adrift, desires ceased.
To welcome a life unseen, unknown,
Embrace the journey to lands unshown.

Letting go is heavy, a burden vast,
Yet clinging to old dreams holds us fast.
It steals our joy, our rightful claim,
To future's bright, free from shame.

Each day unfolds a choice anew,
To follow what the heart deems true.
Persist through trials, face the night,
Hope and prepare for morning's light.

Today can mark a fresh new start,
To trust in life with an open heart.
Leave behind what chains you still,
And rise to meet a better will.

Worth's Voyage

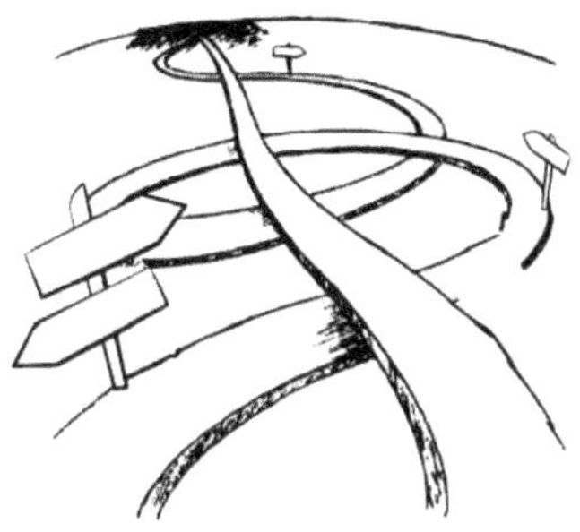

I wish you could fathom your worth,
Of treasures abundant, since your birth.
Good things await, in the wings they wait,
Genuine love, to liberate.

Escape your mind, just for a while,
See all you deserve, with a hopeful smile.
For once glimpsed, once felt, it's true,
You're worthy of all, not just a few.

The echoes of past, they may linger,
But they don't define you, they're not your
singer.
You're worth more than they'd have you believe,
In your heart, that truth, firmly weave.

Open up your heart, let love reside,
Each day a bit more, let love inside.
For as you do, watch the world respond,
All meant for you, journeying on and on.

Acknowledge your worth, embrace it all,
The love, the joy, both big and small.
You're worthy, dear soul, of every part,
Believe it, accept it, let it start.

Choose love wisely….

Choose wisely, for your heart's sake,
Don't settle for less, for love's own sake.
Your person, they'll be there through thick and
thin,
Not just when skies are clear, but also when
storms begin.

Seek someone who's eager to stay,
To walk beside you, come what may.
Support, encouragement, they will freely impart,
Matching your efforts, heart to heart.

Together, you'll laugh, make breakfast, and
more,
For decades on end, forevermore.
Life throws challenges, but love, it's clear,
Should be your solace, in times of fear.

Don't give your all to one who can't see,
The treasure in you, the love that could be.
Hold out for someone who looks your way,
And knows they want forever to stay.

This Kind of love…

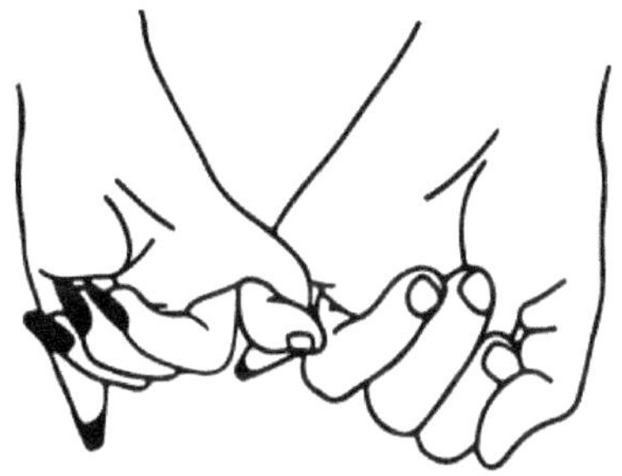

In the quest for love, you deserve the best,
A love that stands out from all the rest.
An "I'll put you first" kind of devotion,
Where nothing else matters, a heartfelt potion.

A hug that lifts you off the ground,
With every embrace, pure joy is found.
A spontaneous drive, just you and me,
"Picking you up, setting your spirit free,
Booking your favourite movie, snacks included too."
Creating moments, letting love grow.

Hand in hand, through life we'll drive,
In every journey, love will thrive.
Arguments may come, but they won't last,
Goodnight kisses, sealing the past.

When sickness strikes, I'll be right there,

With meds, soup, and tender care.
Together, we'll face what comes our way,
Stronger with each passing day.

A love that never wavers, never fades,
Through every challenge, in every shade.
Once in a lifetime, yet forever to last,
A love that changes, a love unsurpassed.

Whispers of compassion

In the quiet corners of my heart, I seek
That gentle love, so tender, yet unique.
A kiss upon my brow, a hug held tight,
My share of affection, in the dimming light.

A soft hand's touch, a guiding hand to hold,
As through life's twists and turns, our paths
unfold.
On buses drifting, in dreams serene,
A shoulder there, a silent, steadfast scene.

In kindness found, unbidden, yet so dear,
A glass of water offered, drawing near.
Removing glasses with a gentle hand,
As words dissolve, and pages softly land.

When fever's flames rage high, and all seems
lost,
A wet cloth soothes, despite the tempest-tossed.
Sharing meals, in tender moments met,
Feeding each other, hearts intertwined, set.

I yearn for more than just the physical toll,
But for my soul, in need of love's console.
A whispered "I love you" at my life's end,
To ease the journey, and hearts to mend.

In that final moment, as shadows creep,
My soul finds solace, in love's embrace deep.
Compassion's touch, a sense of belonging,
A place to rest, in peace, forever longing.

22 Reasons Why…

In the spectrum of reasons to adore yourself,
Here are 22, each one to explore:

1.Your willingness to lend a hand,
Helping others, making their stand.

2.When giving up seems all too near,
You fight on, banishing fear.

3.Kindness and empathy, your guiding light,
Illuminating paths through the darkest night.

4.Your open mind, understanding so vast,
Embracing differences, leaving bias in the past.

5.Persistence, forgiving heart's embrace,
Granting solace, leaving no trace.

6.Resilience and compassion intertwined,
Healing wounds, leaving scars behind.

7.Making all feel at ease, a skill so rare,
Spreading warmth, banishing despair.

8.Loving fully, despite the heart's plea,
Courageous vulnerability, setting love free.

9.Seeing the good in all, through and through,
Unveiling beauty, in every hue.

10.Optimism, a beacon in the storm's gloom,
Planting seeds of hope, in life's vast room.

11.Authenticity, shining bright,
Casting shadows, revealing light.

12.Passion ignites, determination ablaze,
Fueling dreams, in myriad ways.

13.Caring still, when let down by others' deeds,
Forgiving, moving forward, planting seeds.

14.Loyalty's embrace, strength's gentle hold,
Walking side by side, never cold.

15.Growth from challenges, lessons learned,
Wisdom earned, bridges burned.

16.Selflessness, gentleness, tender care,

Nurturing souls, beyond compare.

17.Seeing through another's eyes,
Bridging divides, under endless skies.

18.A friend to lean on, sturdy and true,
A beacon in darkness, guiding you through.

19.Listening ears, time made to spare,
Holding space, showing you care.

20.Showing up, passionate fire aglow,
Pursuing dreams, letting passion flow.

21.Honesty's blade, tempered with love,
Carving truth, from skies above.

22.Striving daily, to be the best you can be,
Unfolding wings, soaring free.
In these reasons, a symphony of love's embrace,
Cherish yourself, in every single space.

Missed Memo

"If the whole world is a stage," they say,
"And everyone's just playing their parts," in a
cliché way,
Then I must've missed the memo, I must've been
late,
When scripts were handed out, sealed by fate.

For everyone seems to know their lines,
Their cues, their marks, their well-rehearsed
designs.
They strut and they prance upon life's grand
stage,
While I stand here, lost, feeling like a sage.

What role do I play? Where do I belong?
I'm like an extra in a play, somehow gone
wrong.
While others deliver their lines with such flair,

I stumble and stutter, unaware.

Damn, I wonder when that meeting was,
Where they dished out instructions, without a
pause.
Perhaps I was napping, or lost in thought,
While others got briefed, and plots were
wrought.

So here I am, in this chaotic scene,
Trying to decipher what it all could mean.
But if life's a play, then let's have some fun,
I'll ad-lib my lines, until my part's done.

Finding Someone

In the journey of life, we seek a soul,
A partner to make our broken pieces whole.
Not one flawless, but filled with love so true,
To weather storms, to see us through.

Finding someone, it's not about perfection's
gleam,
But a heart that sees us, as if in a dream.
Through pain and heartache, they navigate,
Understanding our journey, our burdens great.

It's not mere acceptance, but seeing our light,
Our flaws are embraced, yet love burns bright.
Drowning in love, they learn to float,
Swimming in the depths of our heart's remote.

They know our scars, our inner strife,
Cherishing victories in the battle of life.
Rooting for joy, for happiness untold,
Their love, a shelter from the cold.

Not seeking flawlessness, but a connection so
pure,
A bond that endures, steadfast and sure.
Finding our person, hand in hand we stand,
Saying, "I've journeyed far, through shifting
sand."

They grasp our journey, our trials, our fears,
And in their eyes, we see crystal-clear,
That finding someone, it's never about
perfection's hue,
But about finding the one who truly understands
you.

Apologies

Blame is a torch we often wield,
Accusing others for the wounds unhealed.
Yet in the mirror's gaze, we must confess,
The true culprit lies within, in our own mess.

For every wrong turn, every choice made blind,
It was I, me, myself, who left my peace behind.
Allowing others to break and betray my trust,
Believing their lies, letting them unjust.

Apologies are due, not to another soul,
But to myself, for failing to make me whole.
For not choosing wisdom, for staying naive,
For granting chances to those who deceive.

I apologise for not loving me enough,
For seeking acceptance outside, in the rough.
It's time to prioritise my own well-being,
To guard my soul, my joy, my inner seeing.

No longer will I seek validation from afar,
For within me lies the brightest star.
I vow to cherish myself, to love without
restraint,
And in doing so, break free from self-reproach's
taint.

This Year I turned 40....

I have seen them all, the teens, the twenties, and the thirties,
Been a rebel, an idiot, and wiser, thought it all.
We danced through summer nights, carefree and flirty,
Fell in love, faced heartbreak, stood tall after the fall.

In our teens, the world was a playground vast and wide,
Every moment an adventure, with nothing to hide.
We chased dreams under starry skies, unbound and free,
Believing in forever, in what we could be.

The twenties came like a whirlwind, a time to
explore,
We left home, found new places, and wanted
more.
The city lights beckoned, and we answered the
call,
Learning, failing, loving, and through it all,
standing tall.

Thirties brought clarity, a new depth to our sight,
Balancing ambition with the quiet of night.
We built careers, some built families, and forged
our way,
Learning to cherish the little things each day.

And now we've turned forty, a milestone grand,
With the wisdom of years, a life well-planned.
We've seen the spectrum of joy and of sorrow,
Embracing today while dreaming of tomorrow.

The lines on our faces tell stories untold,
Of laughter, of tears, of memories bold.
We've learned that life's a journey, not a race to
win,
And true beauty lies in the love within.

So here's to the forties, to the paths we've yet to
tread,

To the dreams we'll still chase, the books to be read.
We've been rebels, and idiots, and wise through it all,
And with grace, we embrace the decades yet to call.

www.ingramcontent.com/pod-product-compliance
Lightning Source LLC
LaVergne TN
LVHW050920200726
843508LV00011B/2239